Praise for
Safe Arms

These poems are heart quickening, cinematic, grown. Shout out to Pablo Neruda's lushness, to E. E. Cumming's precision, to Audre Lorde's transformational eroticism. There is an amen here. A call and response, yes. But more than that, these poems acknowledge the holiness of a hand. An intention to pleasure, yes. But also to see. And to be seen.

> — **Imani Tolliver**, Black feminist and queer poet,
> author of *Runaway* A Memoir in Verse

Peter J. Harris is an exciting and welcome new voice. He's got greatness in him. He's got love in him. He's got a lifetime of knowledge for what the soul needs.

> — **Luis Alberto Urrea**, author of *The House of Broken Angels*

Almost 100 years ago, Pablo Neruda created 20 poems of love that re-imaged the oldest, most complex human emotion. Peter J. Harris now gifts us with even more intense and incandescent poems to renew and re-energize expressions of love. The Spanish translations are rich, impressive. A joy to read in a time of uncertainty and pandemic.

> — **Luis and Trini Rodriguez**, co-founders of Tia Chucha's Centro
> Cultural & Bookstore and *The Hummingbird Cricket Hour* podcast

All in! These poems are all in, steaming from wasabi and raw vulnerability that glow in all languages. Peter Harris is committed to the sensuality and deep well-dive of love that is irresistible passion and completeness. As readers, we are voyeurs, tongue hanging, observing tantalizing intimacy. Yes!

> — **Opal Palmer Adisa**, co-editor, *Caribbean Erotic*, anthology
> *(co-edited with Donna Aza Weir-Soley), Professor Emeritus at California*
> *College of the Arts, University Director of the Institute for Gender and*
> *Development Studies at The University of the West Indies*

Oh, yes. *Safe Arms: 20 love & erotic poems* — this bilingual book of love poems by Peter Harris has constructed word on word, mouth on mouth, boca a boca. We journey through erotic feeling and human affection in a language that is both direct and delicate. He/his speaker says "*Give Me Magic*," but we are the ones receiving it. They are the rhythm section of what we understand by the word love. With these poems we get "*lyrics soaked in pot liquor drained from chitlins.*" Gift this. Open some wine. "*Don't tell me shit about Wednesday*," instead glide into places safe, tender, electric and aroused. It takes admirable courage to convey such warmth, such lyricism out of a timeless life. Safe Arms must be held, embraced, read and reread like good love-making, left always on simmer.

— **Lory Bedikian**, *The Book of Lamenting*,
2010 Philip Levine Prize for Poetry

— **William Archila**, *The Gravedigger's Archaeology*,
2013 Letras Latinas/Red Hen Press Poetry Prize

Here we experience food, music, languages, and intelligence (and of course, body, mind, and spirit) as erotic and a source of love. Harris is masterful with the lyric, imagination, and attention. Few poets could or would be able to write this book. This is Neruda for the twenty-first century: bold, pure, and tender in its loving and wonder. The poems, like love and eroticism themselves, feel both timeless and current. The Spanish translations are compassionate, and, if we're talking about the universality of desire, essential. Ultimately, this is a powerful, moving read.

— **Lee Herrick**, author of *Scar and Flower*

Peter Harris' *Safe Arms* is a bilingual chorus of sacred *erotic* songs sung inside a sensual temple where desire is prayer and love is god.

— **Aida Salazar**, author, *The Moon Within, Land of the Cranes,
Voices from Our Ancestors: Xicanx and Latinx Spiritual Expressions
and Healing Practices*

Peter J. Harris delivers a sensual gospel in the way these poems create sanctuary for you. There is a sensual rhythm here and so much beautiful nostalgia. This is that good lovin'. That good love that puts a pep in your step and has your friends questioning your glow. *Safe Arms* holds you and calls you by your name. It excites you. Read this to and with yourself. Read this with a lover after or during the storm. Read this when your body calls for resurrection. *Safe Arms* reminds you that the fight for love is just as important as the fight for freedom.

— **Jasmine Williams**, Executive Director and Host of *Da Poetry Lounge*

Seek into the ache of Marvin's climactic "Oh" and find Peter J. Harris's delirious eros. Only a poet who's made a wild, devotional study of joy could well such deep pleasure with this much Black abandon. Here, find delight and the lit magic of "blackberry music." Play it with your body open.

— **Douglas Kearney**, author of *Buck Studies* and winner of the Theodore Roethke Memorial Poetry Award

Safe Arms

20 love & erotic poems
(w/an *Ooh Baby Baby* moan)

FLOWERSONG
PRESS

poems by
Peter J. Harris

Spanish translation by
Francisco Letelier

FLOWERSONG
PRESS

FlowerSong Press
Copyright © 2022 by Peter J. Harris
ISBN: 978-1-953447-84-5
Library of Congress Control Number: 2021947668

Published by FlowerSong Press
in the United States of America.
www.flowersongpress.com

Cover Design by Francisco Letelier
Author Photo by Tiffany Judkins
Set in Adobe Garamond Pro

NOTICE: SCHOOLS AND BUSINESSES
FlowerSong Press offers copies of this book at quantity discount with bulk
purchase for educational and business use. For information, please email the
Publisher at info@flowersongpress.com.

Brazos Seguros

20 poemas de amor & erótica
(con un gemido *Ooh Baby Baby*)

FLOWERSONG
PRESS

poemas por
Peter J. Harris

Traducción al Español de
Francisco Letelier

w/respect to **Pablo Neruda's** *Veinte Poemas de Amor y una Cancion Desesperada (20 Love Poems and a Song of Despair)*

w/thanks to writers of the Anansi Writers Workshop at The World Stage, Leimert Park, Los Angeles

w/ thanks to contributors and subscribers to *Drumming Between Us: Black Love & Erotic Poetry*, a Los Angeles magazine [1994 to 1999]

Con respeto para *20 Poemas de Amor y una Canción Desesperada* por **Pablo Neruda** *(20 Love Poems and a Song of Despair)*

con agradecimiento por los escritores de el Taller de Escritores Anansi en El World Stage, Leimert Park, Los Angeles

con agradecimiento a los contribuidores y subscriptores a *Tamborileando Entre Nosotros: Amor Negro y Poesía Erótica* una revista de Los Angeles (1994-1999)

Safe Arms

Brazos Seguros

CONTENTS

CONTENIDO

ARCH   TREMBLE   YIELD | An Introduction

By Peter J. Harris

Fingerpaint arousal
Summon delicacy
Shield tenderness
Slay envy
Resurrect mystery
Cradle risk
Sanctify power
Investigate desire's democracy
Embroider Kama Sutra
Litigate taboo
Transcend pornography
Liberate spontaneity
Sing praisesongs
Blush brazenly
Coil religiously
Plunge deliciously
Brave vertigo
Arch
Tremble
Yield

lose all / risk again

ARQUEAR TEMBLAR E N T R E G A R / Una Introducción

Por Peter J. Harris

Exitación de pintura de dedos
Convocar delicadez
Proteger ternura
Matar envidia
Resucitar misterio
Acunar riesgo
Santificar poder
Investigar la democracia del deseo
Bordar Kama Sutra
Litigar tabú
Trascender pornografía
Liberar espontaneidad
Cantar canciones de alabanza
Enrojecerse descaradamente
Enroscarse religiosamente
Zambullirse deliciosamente
Vértigo Valiente
Arqueamos
Temblamos
Entregamos

perder todo / arriesgar de nuevo

#1   Timeless Life

you braid your hair
with a comb of cactus teeth

stroking gel & laughter from the prickly straws
releases the passing days from your face

when your eyelashes rest
& you feel guidance coming on
you bundle dry thorns
& coax a fire from the kindling

you burn fresh-cut herbs
to clean the air & fill my head with aching fantasies

you read the smoke & tell time without a clock
inhale the night   exhale faces hovering over the flames

you sift the rattle of the wind for necessary intervention
we no longer cry   speak only in riddles & proverbs

> this is the timeless life
> I am the timeless seeker
> of a holy woman possessed by
> sight & love & patience   the salvation
> of water & amber & touch

> this is the timeless life
> I am the timeless seeker
> of a holy sister nourished by
> starlight & spiritflight & incantation   the salvation
> of clay & onyx & touch

> this is the timeless life
> I am the timeless seeker
> of a holy lover blessed by
> praise & desire & delight   the salvation
> of smile & truth & touch

#1   Vida sin Tiempo

Te trenzas el pelo
con un peine dientes de cactus

acariciando gel y risa de las pajas espinosas
se sueltan de tu cara los dias que pasan

cuando descansan tus pestañas
y sientes que viene orientación
haces bultos de espinas secas
y halagas un fuego de las astillas

quemas hierbas recien cortadas
para limpiar el aire y llenar mi cabeza con fantasias adoloridas

lees el humo y sin reloj sabes la hora
inhalas la noche exhalas caras flotando encima de las llamas

sorteas el cascabeleo del viento por intervencion necessaria
ya no gritamos   hablamos solo en adivinanzas & proverbios

       esta es la vida sin tiempo
       soy el buscador sin tiempo
       de una mujer santa poseida por
       vista & amor & paciencia   la salvación
       del agua & el ambar & el tocar

       esta el la vida sin tiempo
       soy el buscador sin tiempo
       de una hermana santa nutrida por
       luz de estrellas & vuelo del espiritu & incantación   la salvación
       de greda & onyx & el tocar

       esta es la vida sin tiempo
       soy el buscador sin tiempo
       de una amante sagrada bendecida por
       alabanzas & deseo & delicia   la salvación
       de sonrisa & verdad & el tocar

you set a table for a banquet of cactus meat
you perfume your skin with the spring flower between the quills

you douse the fire with libation
invoked in the language of humility & awe
this is the timeless life
      I am the holy seeker of a timeless woman

dancing within embers of the dying shadows
dancing within stiletto shadows of the cactus flower

pones una mesa para un banquete de carne de cactus
te perfumas la piel con la flor primaveral entre las púas

ahogas el incendio con libación
invocada en el lenguaje de humildad & asombro
esta es la vida sin tiempo
      Soy el buscador bendito de una mujer sin tiempo

bailando dentro de brasas de las sombras moribundas
bailando con las sombras stiletto de la flor de cactus

#2   What I Ask For

an optic nerve of streaking tie-dye   20-20 crystal balls
sudden dawn of a Homeboy in phase with his unfolding religion

I *am* careful what I ask for
knowing that in my pulsing hungers
I will tap the glass eye of a gimp compass
I will follow crumbs of moldy Wonder Bread
to find the vanilla-scented home
of the Sugarcane Priestess
who sweetens my hopeful delirium

She is ancient   understands unspoken posture of my need
She is so hip   realigns round shoulders of my magic

what if your unrehearsed appearance
heralds the age of destination?

what if the unfolding shadows of your cane-cloth wrap
the dance to your music
siphons the source of my indigo moods?

what if your accelerated touch
        the stroke of silken intelligence
can lance the melancholy hovering over me
                                        since time began?

#2   Lo Que Pido

un nervio optico de tie-dye corrido   bolas de cristal 20-20
madrugada repentina de Homeboy en fase con su religion en desarollo

Soy cuidadoso con lo que pido
sabiendo que en mis hambres pulsantes
le daré golpecitos al ojo de vidrio de una brujula coja
seguiré las migas del mohoso pan Bimbo
para encontrar el hogar olor de vainilla
de la Sacerdotista de la Caña de azucañ
quien endulza mi delirio esperanzado

Ella es tan anciana   entiende la postura sin palabras de mi necesidad
Ella es tan chevere   realiñea hombros redondos de mi magia

y si tu apariencia sin ensayos
anuncia la edad de la destinacion?

y si las sombras desplegadas de tu envoltura de tela de caña
el baile a tu musica
sifona la fuente de mis estados de animo indigo?

y si tu toque acelerado
        el golpe de inteligencia sedosa
puede lanzar la melancolia que flota sobre mi

                                    desde que empezo el tiempo?

#3   Give Me Magic

I've already forgiven you for any transgressions
lapses into suburban complacency or arrogant one two three

I'll make a wish that unseals the bottle of aged truth serum
we keep stashed to sip in celebration of another ritual
we've created to get us over the hump of these original lives we live

I will peer over rims of my concrete Ray Bans
look at you with live eyes revealing furious desperation
of a mind working overtime on a blueprint we could fingerprint
until missing each other is our favorite time of day

    give me magic

my faucet of desire & improvisation
a climate scientist's nightmare

my furnace of irreverence
operating without permit in gleeful violation of all stop codes

I will love so profoundly
    you will die
      your last breath divine echo resurrecting
      your perfect form right before our eyes

my hallelujah calling strangers to gather before you

offer of familiar & flexible shelter   memorable meals
    in their gourmet tales of your vintage wonder
    in welcome tales grateful for restoration of your human being
    in stirring tales climaxing in extravagant waves of praise

#3   Dame Magia

Ya te perdone por cualquier transgresiones
lapsos hacia complacencia suburbana o arogancia uno dos tres

Hare un deseo que destapa la botella del añejo suero de la verdad
cual mantenemos oculto para tomar sorbos en celebracion de otro ritual
que creamos para sobrepasar la joroba de vivir estas vidas originales

mirare sobre los marcos de mis Ray Bans de concreto
te avistare con ojos vivos revelando desperación furiosa
de una mente trabajando tiempo extraordinario en un plano
al cual le podriamos sacar huellas digitales
hasta que echarnos de menos es nuestro tiempo favorito del dia.

    dame magia

mi grifo de deseo e improvisación
la pesadilla del científico climático

mi caldera de irreverencia
operando sin permiso en violación dichosa de todo codigo de parada

amaré tan profundamente
    que morirás
    tu ultimo suspiro eco divino resucitando
    tu forma perfecta justo adelante de mis ojos

mi haleluia llamando a que se unan ante ti los desconocidos

oferta de resguardo familiar y flexible   comidas memorables
    en sus cuentos gourmet de tu cosecha asombrosa
    en cuentos bienvenidos agradecidos por restauración de tu ser humana
    en cuentos conmovedores llegando a climax en olas de extravagantes alabanza

#4   Full Grown

hair on this woman's body

blues crocheted into sun-up cradlesong

I suck my thumb
stretch my baby hands
wishes hum in my palms

my nipples become aching candles

I close my eyes
sway to drone welling
from center of my chosen appetites

my breaths fuse
my sex arcs
my hallucinations whimper

face down swearing my allegiance
fingers tracing wayward strands
beard lost sliding cheek along curving ankle
hand tangled up in breathtaking veil

blurs my oldest incoherence
stirs incandescent *my my my*

I faint standing up

#4   Completamente Crecida

el pelo del cuerpo de esta mujer

> *los blues tejidos en cancion de cuna salida del sol*

chupo mi pulgar
estiro mis manos de bebe
deseos tararean en mis palmas

> *mis pezones se convierten en velas dolorosas*

Cierro mis ojos
meneando al zambullido creciente
del centro de mis apetitos escogidos

mis respiraciones se funden
mi sexo arquea
mis alucinaciones dan quejidos

> *cara abajo jurando mi lealtad*
> *dedos trazando hebras caprichosas*
> *barba perdida resbalanose mejilla a lo largo de tobillo curvante*
> *mano enredada en velo que deja sin aliento*

nubla mi incoherencia mas antigua
revuelve incandescente *mi mi mi*

> *me desmayo parado*

#5   Yoga

face sweltering
in the searing cradle
of your flaring hips
my brave right nipple sizzles a circle
against sloping skin of your sex
nipple hovers over sacred opening
I flatten palms into sheets on either side of your undulating frame
flow w/ your exhale
nuzzling against the center of exhilaration

balance of sanctified water
poise of initiated bodies
kiss of tiniest wetness

bowing into pinpoint of infinity
scorched body delivering virgin skin
into folds of our ancient irradiation
we arch   tremble   yield

#5   Yoga

cara sofocada
en la cuna aguda
de tus caderas encendidas
mi pezon derecho valiente crepita un circulo
contra la piel pendiente de tu sexo
pezon flota sobre apertura sagrada
yo aplasto palmas en sabanas a ambos lados de tu marco undulante
fluyo con tu exhalar
hocicando contra el centro de regocijo.

balance de agua santificada
equilibrio de cuerpos iniciados
beso de humedad pequeñisima

inclinados hacia la posicion exacta de la infinidad
cuerpo chamuscado entregando piel virgen
entre pliegues de nuestra irradiación anciana
nosotros arcqueamos   temblamos   cedemos

#6   Wasabi

shock of wetness on my tongue
screams up my jaw
stings skin inside my mouth
savor delicious voltage like a hypnotized wine maker

burning swirl
taste buds shiver a thousand at a time

seeping *wasabi* wakes my wrestling flesh
into a braid of flame

"I'm going to splash on you"

taste buds swoon a thousand at a time
thirst shoots along length of delighted skin

I sip burning guarantee
reborn
quenched

moaning water
dying me to life
with each blazing swallow

#6   Wasabi

golpe mojado en mi lengua
grita arriba en mi mandibula
pica piel adentro de mi boca
saborea voltaje delicioso como un viñero hipnotizado

remolino quemante
papilas gustativas tiritan mil a la vez

wasabi penetrante despierta mi carne luchadora
volviendose en trenza de llama

"Te voy a salpicar"

papilas gustativas se desmayan mil a la vez
sed dispara a lo largo de piel encantada

sorbo garantia quemante
renacido
aplacado

agua de quejas
muriendo me a la vida
con cada trago flameante

#7   Offering

schooled by how you touch yourself
beloved pressure of fingertips webbed by instigating lilt
aha soaking wandering hands
fluttering cries widen your mouth
wonderful sensation circulated
devotional pressure answering your *amen*
ravenous hesitation surging
ceremony when you touch yourself
witness inches from your celebration
mouth faithful at your command
Ashe burns in your offering

#7   Ofrenda

adiestrado por como te tocas
amada presion de las puntas de dedos palmeados por ritmo instigador
aha remojando manos errantes
llantos aleteados enanchan tu boca
sensación maravillosa circulada
presion devocional atendiendo tu *amen*
voraz vacilacion creciente
ceremonia cuando te tocas
el testigo a pulgadas de tu celebración
boca fiel a sus ordenes
Ashe quema en tu ofrenda

#8   Rising Come

consensual arousal slows my evaporation
initiates me into empathetic fusion

kiss flares hydrogen along our lips
oxygen hisses from our craving

I cannot fathom concussion of our rising come

listen to raging weightless above our heads
pull me under & save my life

#8   Venir Creciente

excitación consensual reduce mi evaporación
me inicia hacia fusión empatética

beso enciende hidrógeno a lo largo de nuestros labios
oxígeno sisea desde nuestra ansia

No puedo sondear el golpe de nuestro amanecente venir

escucha la furia ingrávida encima de nuestras cabezas
tirame para abajo & salvame la vida

#9   Recipe

you have seesawed me to rest on my back
curled up in the cradle of my chest
we are a miracle of silence & breath
        I forget how to kiss you
sinking in chemical overtones
wishing before I seep into your scalding mouth
for a recipe I could follow

breathe deeply   forget my past
swallow fear   wait wait

now I remember
invented again by the wizardry of your tongue
a naked man laid down in harmony
who know *damn* well
the only formula that matter
proven mouth on mouth
only passed down
when satisfaction received   satisfaction given

you have undressed
laid me to rest
lit this place
with silence & breath
emptied me in the space before you
memorized me whole with one flickering glance
cooked me within an inch of my life
licked your lips
then helped yourself

#9   Receta

Me haz columpiado hasta el descanso de espalda
enroscada en la cuna de mi pecho
somos un milagro de silencio & aliento
                    me olvido como besarte
hundiendome en trasfondos quimicos
deseando antes de penetrar dentro de tu boca escaldada
por una receta que podria seguir

respira profundamente   olvida mi pasado
traga miedo   espera espera

Ahora me acuerdo
inventado de nuevo por los embrujos de tu lengua
un hombre desnudo tendido en armonía
quien sabe *malditamente* bien
la unica formula que importa
probada boca a boca
solamente transmitida
cuando satisfacción recibida   satisfacción entregada

te has desvestido
me has puesto a descansar
encendido este lugar
con silencio & aliento
me vaciaste en el espacio delante de ti
me memorizaste entero con un vistazo parpadeante
me cocinaste hasta centimetros de mi vida
lamaste tus labios
y entonces te serviste a ti misma

Shadow Below

hides her right hand
in the shadow below her belly button
teases the *shekere'* between her open legs
hips jolted by individual music
playful smile hips me to independent surrender

slide my invitation into her salsa
dip my hips with swagger subsonic
as a Chitlin Circuit rhythm section
sloping bodies curve into each other
like pussy willows blown from inflamed saxophones

I beg her   teach me Spanish with your tongue in my ear
stroke Chinese sign language along my tingling lips

I lick Arabic from right to left across her steaming chest
stutter in shuddering Japanese in time
with the gliding of our indented bodies
we exhale Yoruba into the satisfaction of glistening arms

laugh out loud
after another exhilarating vocabulary lesson

sing a babbling version of Shorty Long's *Function at the Junction*
jab our middle fingers toward the ceiling
to shoot down the helicopter shredding our skin deep revue
kiss until our sanity drowns out the sky
her right hand hovers near my nose
I am hypnotized
slip my left hand into the shadow below her belly button
lose track of common sense   education
& my social security number
return with her to the craving place
where the only documents
have already been signed   sent downtown
& lost in the system

Sombra Debajo

esconde su mano derecha
en la sombra bajo su ombligo
tenta el *shekeré* entre sus piernas abiertas
caderas golpeadas por musica individual
sonrisa jugetona me señala hacia rendimiento independiente

resbalo mi invitacion hacia su salsa
ladeo mis caderas con pavoneo tan subsonico
como sección de ritmo del *Circuito Chitlin*
cuerpos inclinados curvan uno hacia el otro
como sauce de gatito soplado por saxofón inflamado

yo le ruego   enseñame Español con tu lengua en mi oido
traza lenguaje de signos Chino a lo largo de mis labios hormigueantes

yo lamo Arabe de derecha a izquiera a traves de su pecho humeante
tartamudeo en tiempo Japones escalofriante
con el planeo de nuestros cuerpos indentados
exhalamos Yoruba dentro de la satisfacción de brazos radiantes

rio en voz alta
despues de otra leccion de vocabulario estimuladora

cantamos una version balbuceada de *Function at the Junction* de Shorty Long
damos golpes hacia el techo con los dedos del medio
para echar abajo el helicoptero haciendo triturando nuestro show de piel profunda
besamos hasta que nuestra cordura ahoga el cielo
su mano derecha se acerca a mi nariz
estoy hipnotizado
resbalo mi mano izquierda dentro de la sombra debajo de su ombligo
pierdo pista de sentido común   educación
& mi numero de seguro social
vuelvo con ella al lugar de ansia
donde los unicos documentos
ya se han firmado   mandados al centro
& perdidos en el sistema

nobody can punch us up on their computer screens
nobody ever hears from us again
we are never even missed

nadie nos puede encontrar con sus pantallas de computadora
nadie jamas escucha de nosotros
nunca ni nos echan de menos

#11   Only Wine

juice from a blackberry squeezed between my teeth
stains the *shekeré* pulsing between your open legs
sweetens the only wine I ever drink

my face red as when I saw my mother naked for the first and last time
her bra poised in both hands as I barged into her & daddy's room
to say good morning & goodbye
in a high school minute turned eternal moment
her shocked shout & my *"sorry sorry"* an embarrassing memory
that slamming their door has never dimmed

poised at your cinnamon crossroads I can hear taboo voices
haunting me when I'm a mouthful of berry away from mothering you
with kiss so distilled it sweetens the only liquor
this son of an alcoholic father will ever drink

I cannot stay sober sipping the blackberry music of our friction
thirsting for liquid seeping from the source of all beatitudes
aching for my name spoken in your slurred alphabet
helpless as I spill all over the quilt we become
your massaging fingers dissolving me into your body

blessed be the laughter of lovers for it serrates the edges of the future
          bless me with your laughter
blessed be the wine of lovers for it splashes & gives birth to syncopation
          bless me with your wine
blessed be the music of lovers for it seasons the taste of all creation
          bless me with your music

#11   Solo Vino

jugo de una mora exprimido entre mis dientes
mancha el *shekeré* pulsando entre tus piernas abiertas
endulza el único vino que bebo

mi cara roja como cuando vi a mi madre desnuda por primera y última vez
su sostén suspendido en ambas manos cuando irrumpí en la pieza suya y de papá
para decir buenos días y adiós
en un minuto de secundaria convertido en momento eterno
su grito sorprendido y mi "perdón perdón" un recuerdo vergonzoso
que el portazo de sus puertas nunca ha atenuado

suspendido en tu encrucijada de canela, puedo escuchar voces tabú
embrujandome cuando estoy a un bocado de bayas de cuidarte
con un beso tan destilado que endulza el único licor
este hijo de padre alcohólico beberá

no puedo quedarme sobrio bebiendo la música mora de nuestra fricción
sediento por líquido filtrandose por la fuente de todas las bienaventuranzas
adolorido por mi nombre pronunciado en tu alfabeto arrastrado
indefenso mientras derramo sobre la colcha en la cual nos convertimos
tus dedos masajeandome desolviendome en tu cuerpo

bendita sea la risa de los amantes porque asalta los bordes del futuro
      bendíceme con tu risa
bendito sea el vino de los amantes porque salpica y da a luz a la síncopa
      bendíceme con tu vino
bendita sea la música de los amantes porque sazona el sabor de toda la creación
      bendíceme con tu música

#12   My Whole Sky

your eyes control the drift of clouds
wink
strips of cirrus curl toes in shameless anticipation
glare
banks of nimbus growl like a bouncer demanding after-hour passwords

wait a minute now
your whisper slurs the angle of my own orbit
laugh
predictable tides gossip fluently across time zones
frown
conspiratorial stones plot avalanches the first of every month

that aint all
you could will me to take off my clothes
one angular word or insinuating look from you
I'd show you my whole sky   my whole sky
twilight   constellations   heaven
hover over you with an atmosphere of oxygen
solarized by John Coltrane's devotional harmony
you could lie on your back
head propped by sunrise
feet dangling over the settling day

listen
you will hear your favorite birdsong
when I clear my throat
or you could fly in my arms
you cannot fall   I am everywhere
the sky is there   full of your eyes   full of obedient clouds
spangled aurora crowned by preening North Star

navigation?   salvation?

will you command gale or breeze to defrost
the everyday from our dazzling astronomy?

#12   Mi Cielo Entero

tus ojos controlan la deriva de nubes
guiñada
tiras de cirro rizan dedos de los pies en anticipacion desvergonzada
mirada fulminante
bancos de nimbo gruñen como un matón demandando contraseña fuera de
horas

esperate un minuto
tu susurro borra el angulo de mi orbita
riza
mareas previsibles chismean fluidamente atraves de zonas de hora
ceño
piedras conspiradoras complotan avalancha el primero de cada mes

eso no es todo
podrías usar tu voluntad para quitarme la ropa
una palabra angular o una mirada insinuante tuya
Te mostraría mi cielo entero   mi cielo entero
crepúsculo   constelaciones   el paraíso
flotan sobre ti con atmósfera de oxígeno
solarizado por la armonía devocional de John Coltrane
podrías acostarte de espaldas
cabeza apoyada por el amanecer
los pies colgados sobre el día que se asienta

escucha
escucharás tu canto de pájaro favorito
cuando me aclaro la garganta
o podrías volar en mis brazos
no puedes caer   estoy en todas partes
el cielo está alli   lleno de tus ojos   lleno de nubes obedientes
aurora adornada con lentejuelas coronada por Estrella del Norte que se arregla

¿navegación?   ¿salvación?

¿ordenarás tempestad o brisa para descongelar
lo cotidiano de nuestra reluciente astronomía?

#13   Shapeshifter's Groove

B.B. King is a vegetarian
I am your favorite palomino
ride me til I rear up & weep like an electric guitar
swear there are 92 days in a week

on day 41   look down at me
panting in your galloping whirlpool
ask yourself   *how often do I touch a man to tears?*
cup your hands under my eyes   splash my blues on your face
my songs wash down past your breasts
pool between your parachuting legs   soaking our laughing hips

I breathe in fear that you will stop
you breathe easy & familiar as BB's beloved Lucille

then you shift from kneel to crouch to swallow my swelling
squeeze forever out of me
like the love dictator you know I want you to be
at foaming revivals like this

don't tell me shit about Wednesday being *oh happy day*

who could have known BB King was a vegetarian?
guitar propped on his Tony Roma ribs
picking strings   teasing forever out of atmosphere & electricity
nodding in tobacco haze   horns sizzling like a Whopper getting grilled
lyrics soaked in pot liquor drained from chittlins
appetite voracious as a buccaneer raising mutton after mutiny
pork chop backbeat goading me to close my eyes
surrender to songs old as my father's bootlegger memories
embossing my loneliness   teaching me to beg
stinging my ear like you biting & hissing that
I better come or you will stop pinching my nipples
stop pounding me into grateful agony
stop gripping me with your womb
snatch your delicious from my salivating mouth
wipe that rapture off my face

#13   Groove De Cambiaformas

B.B. King es vegetariano
yo soy tu palomino favorito
móntame hasta que me alzo y lloro como guitarra eléctrica
juro hay 92 días en una semana

el día 41 mírame por encima
jadeando en tu remolino galopante
pregúntate *con qué frecuencia toco a un hombre hasta las lágrimas?*
pon tus manos debajo de mis ojos   salpica mis blues en tu cara
mis canciones lavan más allá de tus senos
hacen charco entre tus piernas paracaídas empapando nuestras caderas rientes

Respiro con miedo que te detengas
tu respiras tranquila & familiar como la amada Lucille de BB

entonces pasas de rodillas al agacho para tragar mi hinchazón
exprí me el siempre de mi
como el dictador del amor que sabes que quiero que seas
en espumosos avivamientos como este

no me digas mierda que el miércoles es *oh día feliz*

quién podría haber sabido que BB King era vegetariano?
guitarra apoyada en sus costillas Tony Roma
tocando cuerdas   provocando el siempre de la atmósfera & electricidad
asintiendo en la bruma del tabaco   cuernos chisporroteando como
Whopper a la parrilla
letras empapadas en licor de olla colado de menudo
apetito tan voraz como bucanero criando cordero tras motín
ritmo de fondo chuleta de chancho aguijandome a cerrar los ojos
rendirme a canciones viejas como los recuerdos contrabandistas de mi padre
estampando mi soledad   enseñandome a rogar
picandome la oreja como si mordiendo & siseando que
mejor que me venga o pararás de pellizcarme los pezones
pararás de golpearme en agonía agradecida
pararás de agarrarme con tu seno
arrebataras tu delicia de mi boca salivada
limpiar ese gozo de mi cara

what can I do under such torture?
you are the love dictator
we too far gone into shapeshifter's groove

I am your skittish palomino   I rear up weeping
you ride me bareback til I plead
there are 92 days in every week
& I don't ever want this work to end

qué puedo hacer bajo tal tortura?
eres la dictadora del amor
hemos llegado demasiado lejos en el groove del cambiaformas

soy tu palomino asustadizo   me alzo en dos patas llorando
me montas a pelo hasta que declaro
hay 92 días en cada semana
& no quiero que termine este trabajo jamas

#14   Something Ferocious, Something Delicious

on sidewalks   in the marketplace   as humble pedestrians
    we are talk
blending language to our bidding
grammar   syntax muffled with common terms
common signs   common meanings

> *up under*
> *shuddering   shattering*
> *we are acoustic genius moaning*
> *wordless surging promises*
> *throbbing autobiography*
> *something ferocious   something delicious*

let other people dwell on their helpless surfaces
kneel & pray to hear the drumming between us
covet the sound circling from our fluent & chemical skin
their protocol & hesitation complicated by our patent leather disdain

our promenade is syncopated teasing
cunning beats scratched from suspense amplify our multiplication
other people go insane surging & swooping to our Fandango
still beg to hum the music emanating from our deep & wordless jam

wrong ears burn at the music we compose
sun blinds spies trafficking gossip about us
wind sweeps away the memories of people who mean us harm
mountains crumble warnings to any with prying disposition

> *alone within our consecrated circumference*
> *whirlpools leap from a cappella proverbs   falsetto water bubbles*
> *ferocious drumming delicious between us*
> *our reverberating momentum is a choir at rest*

#14   Algo Feroz, Algo Delicioso

en las aceras en el mercado   como humildes peatones
    somos el hablar
mezclando lenguaje a nuestras ordenes
gramatica sintaxis amortiguados con términos comunes
signos comunes   significados comunes

> *arriba debajo*
> *estremecimiento estremecedor*
> *somos genio acústico gimiendo*
> *oleada de promesas sin palabras*
> *palpitante autobiografía*
> *algo feroz   algo delicioso*

deja que otras personas se detengan en sus superficies indefensas
arrodíllen & rezen para escuchar el tamboreo entre nosotros
codicien el sonido circulando desde nuestra piel fluida & química
su protocolo & vacilación complicadas por nuestro desdén de charol

nuestro paseo es burla sincopada
ritmos astutos rayados del suspenso amplifican nuestra multiplicación
otras personas se vuelven locas, surgiendo & arremetiendo a nuestro Fandango
todavía ruegan zumbar la música que emanando
de nuestra zapada profunda & sin palabras

oídos equivocados queman con la música que componemos
sol enciega espías traficando chismeo acerca de nosotros
el viento barre recuerdos de personas que nos quieren hacer daño
montañas desmoronan advertencias a cualquiera con disposición entrometida

> *solo dentro de nuestra circunferencia consagrada*
> *los remolinos saltan de proverbios a-capela   burbujas de agua falsete*
> *tamboreo feroz delicioso entre nosotros*
> *nuestro impulso reverberante es un coro en reposo*

#15   Safe Arms

my voice   her ear
(I speak because she listens
 her frown of concentration
 is a gift that honors & surprises me)
she takes me seriously
lifts me to the heights of the love I need
I hope my voice is Eddie Kendricks in her ear
or whatever falsetto feed her
like she is sound in flesh feed me
& everybody   everyday   *everywhere*
if you ask me

her voice   my need
(because she speaks I catch bullets
 fired from open car windows
 her tears of relief redeem me
 renew my wounded palms)
who could I take more seriously?
shielded by the heights of the love I need

> I bow to become in her lap
> God is in the weight of her hands
> stoking my naked shoulders
> I am a joey in her safe arms
> too old to be born from her body
> but she calls me *baby boo* anyway

now dessert is both her nipples filling my mouth
quaking sounds lift us to the love we need
I am awake with eyes closed like the infant she makes me
trusting in the touch of instinct to temper
my drowning in her newborn skin
serene in my second sight to each memory she breathes
with each time I swallow

no voice   all new
(fulfilling rhythm

#15   Brazos Seguros

mi voz   su oido
(Hablo porque ella escucha
 su ceño de concentración
 es un regalo que me honra y me sorprende)
ella me toma en serio
me eleva a las alturas del amor que necesito
Espero que mi voz sea la de Eddie Kendricks en su oído
o cualquier falsete le de comer
como ella es sonido en carne, dame de comer
& todos todos los días *en todas partes*
si me preguntas

su voz   mi necesidad
(porque ella habla atrapo balas
 disparadas desde ventanas abiertas de vehiculo
 sus lágrimas de alivio me redimen
 renuevan mis palmas heridas)
a quién podría tomar más en serio?
protegido por las alturas del amor que necesito

> me inclino para llegar a ser ambos en su falda
> Dios esta en el peso de sus manos
> avivando mis hombros desnudos
> Soy un joey en sus brazos seguros
> demasiado viejo para nacer de su cuerpo
> pero ella me llama *guaguita linda* de todos modos

ahora el postre son sus dos pezones llenando mi boca
sonidos temblorosos nos elevan al amor que necesitamos
Estoy despierto con los ojos cerrados como el infante que ella me hace
confiando en el toque de instinto para templar
mi ahogamiento en su piel recién nacida
sereno en mi clarividencia a cada recuerdo que ella respira
con cada vez que trago

sin voz   todo nuevo
 (ritmo cumplidor

unshakable as a widow's moan
sacred as an orphan's faith)
bound as if with chemicals distilled from martyrs' tears
eternal alms in her unspoken word
eternal comfort in ark of consecrated embrace

inquebrantable como gemido de viuda
tan sagrado como fe de huérfano)
atado como con químicos destilados de lágrimas de mártires
limosna eterna en su palabra no hablada
consuelo eterno en e arca de abrazo consagrado

#16   **Green**

rain forest slips into your voice
religious leaves
streams from headwaters of all music
holy volume
speak to me   speak to me
silk spools off your teeth
lush & wordless   awake
with grape whispers
with blue poppies
with kaleidoscopic nightspeak

I hush in your arms
witness with no name
palms bow across your path
fronds convert chlorophyll
green whirls within your eyes
fuchsias coil around your touch
blushing & star struck   wet
with grape whispers
with blue poppies
with instigating nightspeak

your kiss   powerful & patient
awake
summoning desire's democracy
speak to me   speak to me
rain splashes off your tongue
alive & renewed   aching
with grape whispers
with blue poppies
with indestructible nightspeak

Verde

la selva tropical se desliza dentro tu voz
hojas religiosas
corrientes desde las cabeceras de toda música
volumen sagrado
háblame   háblame
seda carretea de tus dientes
exuberante & sin palabras   despierto
con susurros de uva
con amapolas azules
con hablar nocturno caleidoscópico

me callo en tus brazos
testigo sin nombre
palmas se inclinan en tu camino
frondas convierten clorofila
verde se remolina dentro de tus ojos
fucsias enrollan alrededor de tu toque
ruborizado & golpeado por estrellas   mojado
con susurros de uva
con amapolas azules
con hablar nocturno instigador

tu beso   poderoso & paciente
despierto
convocando la democracia del deseo
háblame   háblame
lluvia salpica de tu lengua
doliendo   viva & renovada
con susurros de uva
con amapolas azules
con hablar nocturno indestructible

she laugh
sweep away my name
hairs flicker up & down my arms
dare me beyond silly taboos
I can't hide love

maybe I'm sweeter than I think
if she let me in her life   her body
if all this roaming
bouncing 2 lovers' frequency off satellites
short circuit everybody's wet dreams

maybe I'm spilling secrets best left to
beckoning dusk or taunting sunrise
if I tell you she welcome on my lap
legs yawning
head thrown back
spine elegant in limbo
seizure rippling her face
mouth a perfect circle
breath a hypnotizing thrust

telepathy steal her from gravity's arms
guide her whiplash back home
fever mold satin against my chest
sob splash in my face
tears glisten on my mustache
faith suspend us on shivering arms
nothing between us but incandescence

I sink into her geometry
touch magnetize skin
weld hips
suffocate cool
collapse dusk into sunrise
time a wistful peeping tom
braiding his fingers into a sizzling wick
licking sweat off these moments with no shame

Conoce Este Secreto

ella rie
barre mi nombre
pelos parpadean arriba & abajo mis brazos
me desafían más allá de tabúes idiotas
no puedo esconder amor

tal vez soy más dulce de lo que pienso
si ella me dejara entrar en su vida   su cuerpo
si todo este *roaming*
rebotando frecuencia 2 amantes desde satélites
cortacircuito los sueños húmedos de todos

tal vez estoy derramando secretos mejor dejados a
atraer atardecer o burlár amanecer
si te digo que ella es bienvenida en mi falda
piernas bostezando
cabeza tirada para atrás
columna elegante en el limbo
convulsión ondulando su cara
boca un círculo perfecto
aliento un impulso hipnotizante

telepatía la roba de los brazos de gravedad
gui su latigazo de vuelta a casa
satín fiebre moho contra mi pecho
sollozo salpica en mi cara
lágrimas brillan en mi bigote
fe nos suspende en brazos temblorosos
nada entre nosotros sino incandescencia

me hundo en su geometría
toque magentiza piel
soldo caderas
sofoco lo fresco
colapso anochecer convirtiendolo en amanecer
el tiempo un mirón melancólico
trenzando sus dedos en una mecha candente
lamiendo el sudor de estos momentos sin vergüenza

who don't want to know this secret
born in laughter
silly as cartoon TNT
serious as sex at high noon on a Sunday
without prayer religion or sin

quien no quiere saber este secreto
nacido en risa
tonto como dibujos animados TNT
tan serio como sexo al mediodía del Domingo
sin oración religión o pecado

#18   Levitation

this common shore   Arrival Ground   Capital City
of our 10-fingered democracy   home to daybreak mouths   unbuttoned
speech   glowing bodies   dazzling home for citizens ending disrespected
journeys

we rise in the same mornings now
witness flames of intention tiptoe on the surface of time

nothing has a chance of ever being the same
no instrument could measure the pleasure
your boiling visitation brings to me

no eye see   no mouth say
no other who has not loved & left my mother's womb
would I trust to know this new secret about me

we take the oath of office
pledge to uphold the levitation

my right hand raised   testifying
like in church back home

your left hand poised   affirming
as in sacred rites accenting your beloved land

velvet hands   naked shoulders   alliance of vulnerable directions

we crossing latitudes here   unmarked
thick with trees in season
humid with wild gaze   unknowns

around our open throats we drape curiosity
smoothing knots into patterns could cause war in the past

                                    culture changes
when people weave new patterns like this

#18   Levitación

esta costa comun   Campo de Llegada   Ciudad Capital
de nuestra democracia diez dedos hogar de bocas del amanecer desbotonado
discurso cuerpos encendidos hogar resplandiente para ciudadanos terminando irespetuados
viajes

ahora subimos en las mismas mañanas
atestiguamos llamas de intencion puntapie en la superficie del tiempo

nada tiene el azar de siempre ser igual
ningun instrumento podria medir el placer
que trae tu visitación hirviente

ningun ojo ve ni una boca dice
ningun otro quien no ha amado & dejado el seno de mi madre
podria confiar saber este secreto nuevo sobre mi

tomamos el juramento de oficina
comprometemos mantener la levitación

mi mano derecha alzada testificando
como en iglesia de donde soy

tu mano izquierda posada   afirmando
como en los ritos sagrados acentuando tu tierra querida

manos de terciopelo hombros desnudos   alianza de direcciones vulnerables

nosotros aqui cruzando latitudes sin marca
gruesas con arboles en estacion
humedos con mirada salvaje   desconocidos

alrededor de nuestros cuellos colgamos curiosidad
suavizando nudos en patrones que en el pasado podrian causar guerra

cultura cambia
cuando gente teje nuevos patrones asi

feeling ripens
when strangers design new patterns like this

love surprises
when people risk new patterns like this

                    sentimientos maduran
cuando desconocidos diseñan nuevos patrones asi

amor sorprende
                    cuando gente arriesga nuevos patrones asi

#19   Tender Mask

my hand is a tender mask covering her face
song escapes soft lips
reads my lifeline
divines how we will spend the reincarnations our pleasure announces

> *soft lips*
> *divine face*
> *first light*
> *next life*

teeth press into flesh
breath blesses skin
open hands lace
eyelashes slit fingers
kiss sweetens palm
dusts fingerprints
slows sweep of time

> *soft lips*
> *divine face*
> *first light*
> *next life*

> *breathe skin breathe   come song come*
> *breath of singing skin   sing skin sing*
> *skin become song   song become skin*
> *sing skin breathe   breathe skin sing*

#19   Máscara Tierna

mi mano es una mascara tierna cubriendo su cara
cancion escapa labios suaves
lee mi linea de vida
divina como pasaremos las reincarnaciones que anuncia nuestro placer

> *labios suaves*
> *cara divina*
> *primera luz*
> > *proxima vida*

dientes presionan carne
aliento bendice piel
manos abiertas atan
pestañas rajan dedos
beso endulce palma
empolva huellas digitales
disminuye barrida del tiempo

> *labios suaves*
> *cara divina*
> *primera luz*
> > *proxima vida*

> *respira piel respire   ven cancion ven*
> *aliento de piel cantante   canta piel canta*
> *piel se hace cancion   cancion se hace piel*
> *canta piel respira respira piel canta*

#20   Sleep

I am lying behind her
tracing drowsy lips with my forefinger
her tongue
a lazy trombone solo
sips my thumb
glory within our nestling
tasting safety in my clean hand
we are childhood serenity banishing nightmares
shuddering   shattering
reborn under comforter
freedom in our sleep
woman's desire
girl's peace
suckling my thumb
steeping in contentment
sliding along night time's solo
slipping into moist whispers   seashell echoes
woozy witness in the back of her head

#20   Dormir

estoy tendido detras de ella
trazando labios soñolientos con dedo índice
su lengua
un solo flojo de trombon
sorbe mi pulgar
gloria dentro de nuestro acurruceo
saboreando seguridad en mi mano limpia
somos serenidad de niñez desterrando pesadillas
estremecimiento estremecedor
renacidos bajo plumón
libertad en nuestro dormir
deseo de mujer
paz de niña
chupandome el pulgar
empapado en contento
deslizándo a lo largo del solo de noche
resbalando hacia susurros humedos   ecos caracol de mar
testigo mareado detras de su cabeza

10/16/97
(an *Ooh Baby Baby* moan)

it is a full moon   i have just lost the woman i love   i am insane   it is the
end of the world   oxygen is acid on my skin   i commit suicide on the quills
of my down pillow   each breath resuscitates a corpse   the anniversary of my
rejection looms every 7 days   my scrotum sac is as dry as shed snake skin
my penis is a magician's wand that's lost all abracadabra

solder my lips   i will never flood my mouth with the kiss of the woman
i love   novocaine my tongue   i will never trace the ears of the woman i
love   transplant my fingerprints   i will never cradle the hips of the woman i
love   clog my pores   i will never receive the chemistry of the woman i love
shroud the world's mirrors   i will never be beautiful again

i have entered the concentrated time of knowing   i hold my breath & pray
to hear the missing menthol on the altar in her voice   the endorphin circle
has been closed with no invitation   her disappearance is the only eloquence
in this cauldron   now i bathe alone in a clawfoot tub for two filled by my
sobs & the steam does not soothe my deletion

now nightmares shock me awake at 5 in the morning & stunt the yawning
of the dawn   now i wear 2 pairs of hiking boots & limp up and down hills
without even a gimp compass   now i speak monologues to empty chairs &
my throat is an arroyo in august   now progesterone & oxytocin flood my
body & i enter labor with no one to coach my breathing   no one to wipe
sweat off my face   tears off my face   grimace off my face

> *how many fingers & toes will i have when i am reborn?*
> *who will teach me that love is still indispensable?*
> *what will i remember of devastation?*
> *what will i remember of loss?*

i am a fool who must remember what has never existed   i am a singer who
must close his ears to wishful music   i am a beggar who must give away the
gifts he receives   i am a man who must turn his back on the answer to his
prayers   this must be the beginning of the world   your love completes my
genetic code   standing under night sky constellations shift positions until

10/16/97
(un gemido *Ooh Baby Baby*)

es luna llena recien he perdido la mujer que quiero estoy loco es el
fin del mundo oxigeno es ácido en mi piel me suicido en los raquis
de mi almohada de plumas cada respire resucita un cadaver el aniversario de mi
rechazo se cierna cada 7 dias el saco de mi escroto esta tan seco como piel mudada de culebra
mi pene is una varilla de mago que ha perdidido todo abracadabra

suelda mis labios nunca inundare mi boca con el beso de la mujer
que quiero novocaína mi lengua nunca trazare las orejas de la mujer que
quiero transplantar mi huellas digitales nunca acunaré las caderas de la mujer que
quiero obstruye mis poros nunca recibire la quimica de la mujer que quiero
cubran los espejos del mundo nunca seré bello de nuevo

he entrado al tiempo concentrado del saber aguanto respirar & rezo
escuchar el mentol que falta en el altar en su voz el circulo de endorfinas
se ha cerrado sin invitación su desaparición es la unica elocuencia
en esta caldera ahora me baño solo en una bañera patas de garas para dos llena de mis
sollozos & el vapor no alivia mi cancelación

ahora pesadillas me hacen shock despertandome a las 5 de la mañana & atrofian el
bostezo del amanecer ahora uso dos pares de botas hiking & cojeo subiendo y
bajando cerros sin ni un compas tullido ahora hablo monólogos hacia
sillas vacías & mi carganta es un arroyo en agósto ahora progestorona &
oxitocina inunden mi cuerpo & entro el parto sin alguien que me entrene la
respiracion nadie que limpie el sudor mi cara lagrimas mi cara mueca mi cara

cuantos dedos de las manos & dedos de los pies tendre cuando renazco?
quien me enseñara que el amor es aun indispensable?
que me acordaré de la devastación?
que me acordaré de perdida?

Soy un tonto quien se tiene que acordar de lo que nunca existio soy un cantante
quien debe cerrar los oidos a musica ilusionada soy un mendigo quien tiene que
regalar los regalos recibidos soy un hombre que tiene que dar espaldas a las respuestas
de sus rezos esto tiene que ser el comienzo del mundo tu amor completa mi
codigo genético parado bajo cielo de noche constelaciones cambian posiciónes

stars connect to reveal your face   in your presence i taste flavor i cannot
stand to lose   i am satisfied that i smell in you the fragrance of my destiny

but it is a full moon   we have vanished from the flow of time   gaping hope
bleeds down the front of my chest   unsung want twists my posture   helpless
fear jolts my walk into baby steps

i stumble
refuse weapons
swallow the kola nut you have placed on my tongue
volunteer to love despite advice of the bitter child in my eyes
search for the gift
stare at the eclipse

> *hunger for breath // it is a full moon*
> *hunger for faith // i have lost*
> *hunger for life // i am insane*

> *how many toes & fingers?*
> *who is indispensable?*

> *who will bless these ashes*
> *before winter rains wash them to the ocean?*
> *who will bless the devastation*
> *presiding over my naming ceremony?*
> *who will help me erect for eternity*
> *a pyramid of dignity & joy?*

> then dab sweat stinging my lovely face
> then kiss tears staining my loving face
> then melt grimace freezing my beloved face

hasta que estrellas se conectan para revelar tu cara   en tu presencia pruebo sabor
que no puedo soportar perder   estoy satisfecho que huelo en ti la fragancia
de mi destino

pero es luna llena   hemos desvanecido del fluir del tiempo esperanza
abierta sangra por mi pecho el quierer sin cantar tuerce mi postura
miedo indefenso sacude mi caminar transformandolo a pasos de bebé

me tropiezo
rehuso armas
trago la nuez de kola que has puesto en mi lengua
me ofrezco amar a pesar de consejos del niño amargo en mis ojos
busco el regalo
miro fijamente al eclipse

> *hambre por aliento // es luna llena*
> *hambre por fé // he perdido*
> *hambre por vida // estoy loco*
>
> *cuantos dedos de las manos & los pies?*
> *quien es indispensable?*
>
> *quien bendicera estas cenizas*
> *antes que lluvias de invierno las lleven al mar?*
> *quien bendicera la devastacion*
> *presidiendo sobre mi ceremonia de nombramiento?*
> *quien me ayudara erejir para eternidad*
> *un pirámide de dignidad & alegria?*

entonces quita el sudor que pica mi cara adorable
entonces besa lagrimas que manchan mi cara amorosa
entonces derrite mueca que congela mi cara amada

Bio for Peter J. Harris
Writer & Cultural Worker

Peter J. Harris, 2018 Los Angeles COLA Fellow in literary arts, Fellow of the Los Angeles Institute for the Humanities at USC, and award-winning poet/essayist, is the author of *Bless the Ashes*, poetry (Tia Chucha Press), winner of the 2015 PEN Oakland Josephine Miles Award, and *The Black Man of Happiness: In Pursuit of My 'Unalienable Right,'* a book of personal essays, winner of a 2015 American Book Award. In 2022, Beyond Baroque Books will publish Harris' book of poetry *SongAgain*.

Harris is founding director of The Black Man of Happiness Project, *www.blackmanofhappiness.com*, a creative, intellectual and artistic exploration of Black men and joy. Harris writes the blog *WREAKING HAPPINESS: A Joyful Living Journal: www.inspirationcrib.com*.

His 2018 TEDx Pasadena Talk with Adenike A. Harris, at Huntington Library, "Healing vs. Retaliation: Surviving Trauma and Sexual Abuse," described and celebrated 15 years of working with his daughter after convicting and jailing her predator ex-stepfather. Harris and his daughter are also contributors to *Love WITH Accountability: Digging up the Roots of Child Sexual Abuse*, edited by Aishah Shahidah Simmons (2019).

Since the 1970s, Harris has published his work in a wide variety of publications, including *Wide Awake: Poets of Los Angeles and Beyond*, edited by Suzanne Lummis; *Altadena Poetry Anthologies for 2018 and 2019;* and *Coiled Serpent: Poets Arising from the Cultural Quakes & Shifts in Los Angeles*, edited by Neelanjana Banerjee, Daniel A. Olivas, and Ruben J. Rodriguez. Since 1992, Harris has been a member of the Anansi Writers Workshop at the World Stage, in LA's Leimert Park.

Bio de Peter J. Harris
Escritor y Trabajador Cultural

Peter J. Harris, 2018 Los Angeles COLA Fellow en artes literarias y Fellow del Instituto de Los Angeles para las Humanidades en USC, es el autor de *Bless the Ashes*, poesia (Tia Chucha Press), ganador del premio Josephine Miles 2015 PEN Oakland.; y ganador del 2015 American Book Award por *The Black Man of Happiness: In Pursuit of My 'Unalienable Right,'* un libro de ensayos personales. En 2022, Beyond Baroque Books publicará el libro de poesía de Harris *SongAgain*.

Es el director fundador del Proyecto Hombre Negro de Felicidad / The Black Man of Happiness Project, *www.blackmanofhappiness.com*, una exploración creativa, intelectual e artistica de hombres Negros y la alegria. Su blog se llama *Wreaking Happiness: Joyful Living Journal: www.inspirationcrib.com*.

Su charla TEDx Pasadena Talk del 2018, con Adenike A. Harris en la Biblioteca Huntington, "El Sanar vs. Represalias: Sobreviviendo Trauma y Abuso Sexual", decribió y celebró 15 años de trabajo con su hija despues de la condena y encarcelamiento de su depredador ex padrastro.

Desde los años 70, Harris ha publicado su trabajo en una amplia variedad de publicaciones, mas recientemente en *Altadena Poetry Review: Antologia, editada por by Teresa Mei Chuc y Hazel Clayton Harrison; Muy Depiertos: Poetas de Los Angeles y mas Alla*, editada por Suzanne Lummis; *Altadena Poetry Review: Antologia*, editada por Thelma T. Reyna, Poetisa Laureada de Altadena; y Serpiente Enroscada; Poetas levantandose de Temblores y Cambios en Los Angeles, editores Neelanjana Banerjee, Daniel A. Olivas, y Ruben J. Rodriguez. Desde 1992, ha sido miembro del Taller de Escritores Ananzi en el World Stage/ Escenario Mundial en el distrito Parque Leimert de Los Angeles.

Publication History

The following poems, or versions of them, first appeared in the following publications:

Aint No Kiss, Only Wine, Yoga, Wasabi, Offering, Rising Come, Recipe, Shadow Below, Only Wine, Safe Arms, Green, Know This Secret, Tender Mask, Sleep, and **10/16/97** – first edition of the chapbook, *Safe Arms: 20 Love & Erotic Poems (and One Ooh Baby Baby Moan)* (2004, Inspiration House).

Shapeshifter's Groove – *The Antioch Review*, (Fall 2001, Volume 59, Number 4).

10/16/97 (an *Ooh Baby Baby* moan) – *Angels Flight Literary West*, (November 15, 2019).

Publicacion Anterior

Los siguientes poemas o sus verisones aparecieron por primera vex en las siguientes publicaciones:

Solo Vino, Yoga, Wasabi, Ofrenda, Venir Creciente, Receta, Sombra Debajo, Brazos Seguros, Verde, Conoce Este Secreto, Máscara Tierna, Dormir y **10/16/97** – primera edición del chapbook, *Safe Arms: 20 Love & Erotic Poems (and One Ooh Baby Baby Moan)* (2004, Inspiration House).

Groove de Cambiaformas – *The Antioch Review*, (Otoño 2001, Volumen 59, Numero 4).

10/16/97 (un gemido *Ooh Baby Baby*) – *Angels Flight Literary West*, 15 Noviembre, 2019).